Pirate Swears

Swear Word Coloring Book to Rant & Relax

By
I ♥ Coloring Books

Introduction

Aaarrggg Matey, salty sayings that will make a landlubber blush fill the following pages. They are meant for entertainment purposes and to be rude crude and offensive, and there you have it!

Sometimes after a long hard day it feels like you've been keel hauled and made to walk the plank at least a dozen times and you just need a shore pass. You want nothing more than to sit back with an ale, and glass of rum, or some other beverage of choice and color all those richly insulting sayings you've been shouting in your head at the blithering idiots around you!

Pirate Swears is the perfect way to unwind and release your inner sailor. Enjoy these irreverent, yet beautiful adult coloring pages. Then sit back and tell the blighters to just Flog Off!

These single sided pages range from moderate to highly detailed and include abstract patterns, ocean themes and more… Each has its own richly authentic swear that, will have you sounding like an 18th century pirate in no time! Sayings like "You've got no more brain than a boil on my arse," "I'll let out your evil soul by incision of steel," and my personal favorite, "Heinous fuckery most foul!"

You'll find these and 22 other humorous, salty sayings to expand your inappropriate vocabulary and help you de-stress and relax!

Enjoy!

I ♥ Coloring Books

Color Test Page

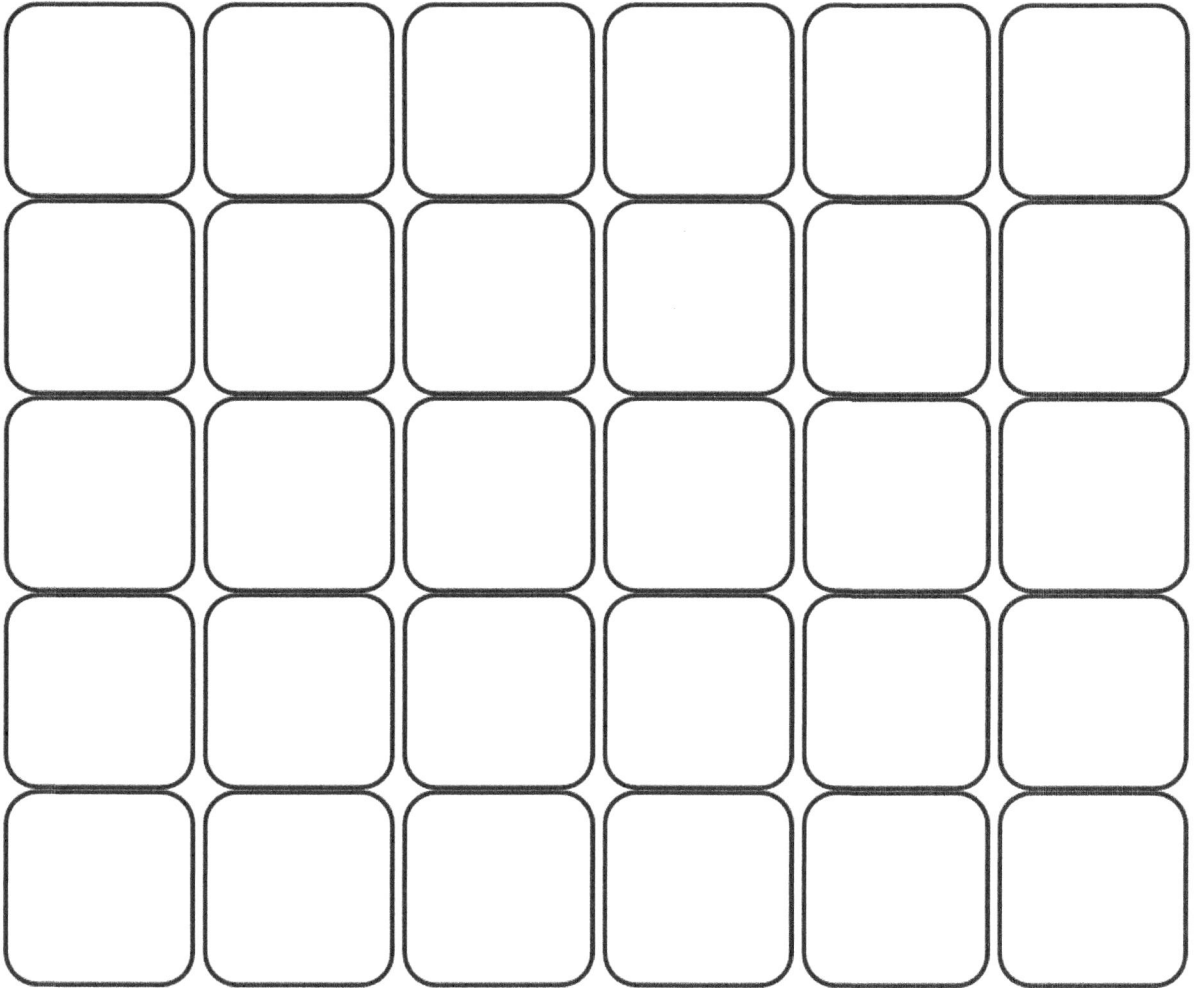

Color Test Page

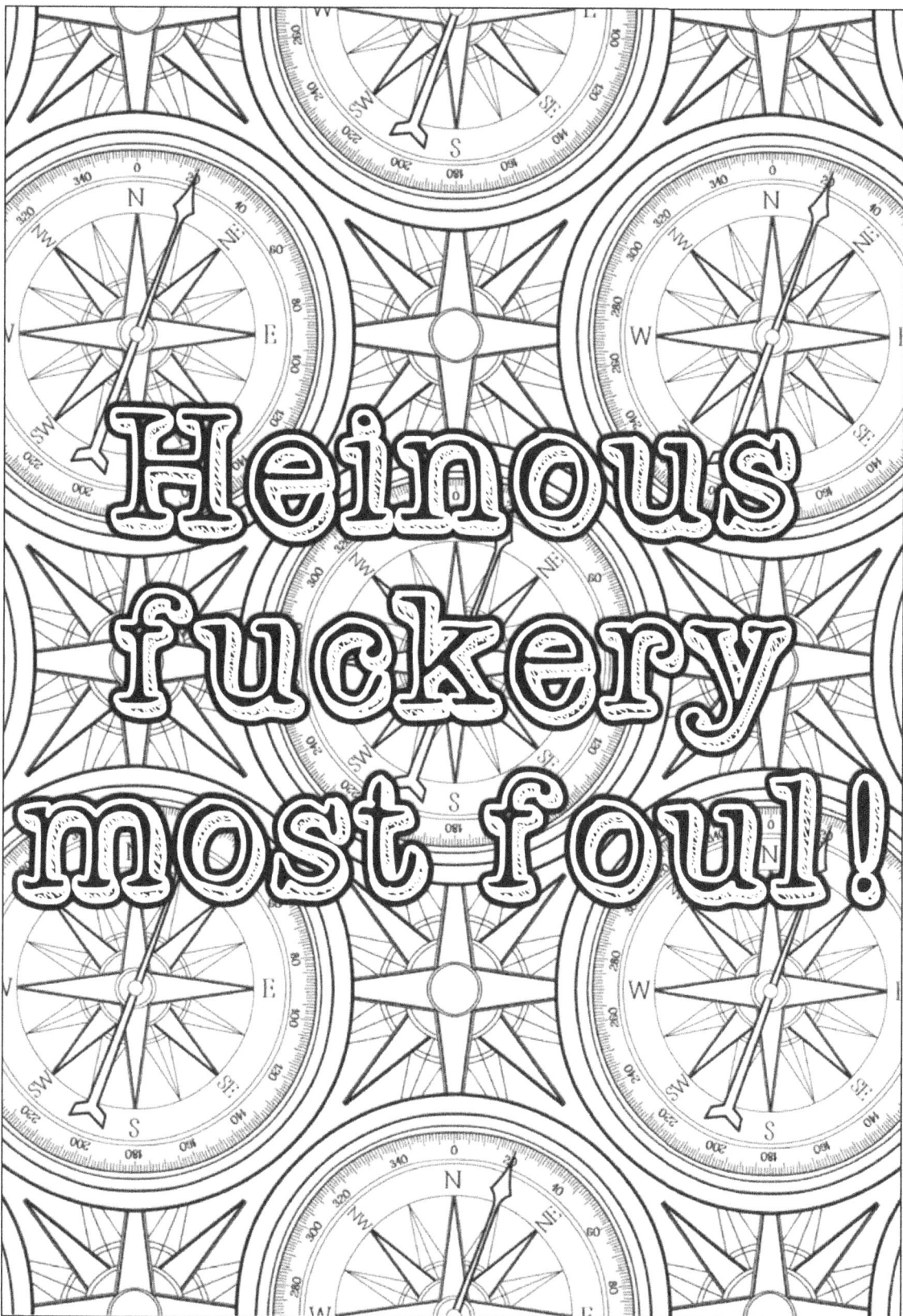

Heinous fuckery most foul!

YOU GLUTTONOUS WHORE

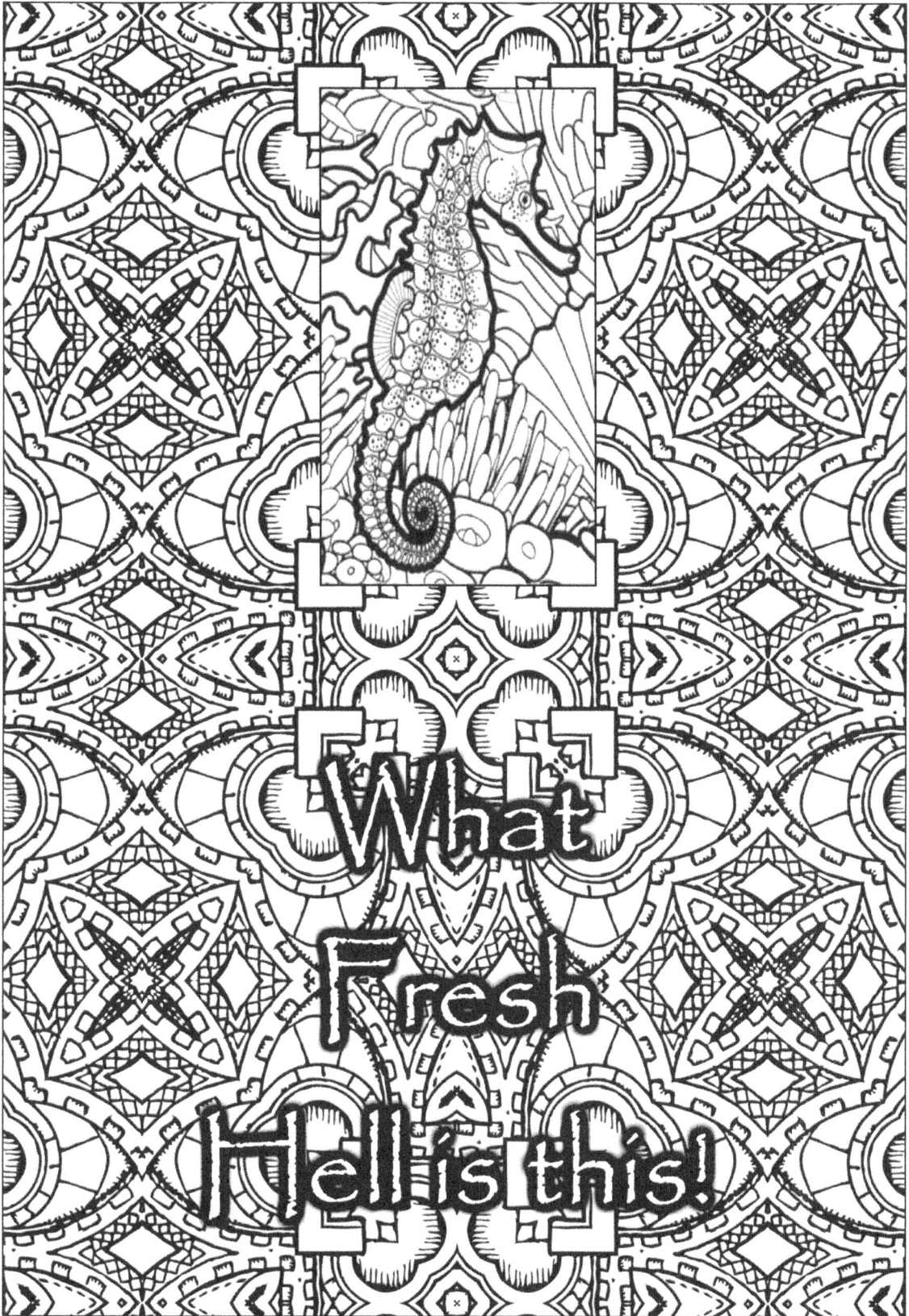

What
Fresh
Hell is this!

I bite my thumb at thou

He Be Drunk as a Lord

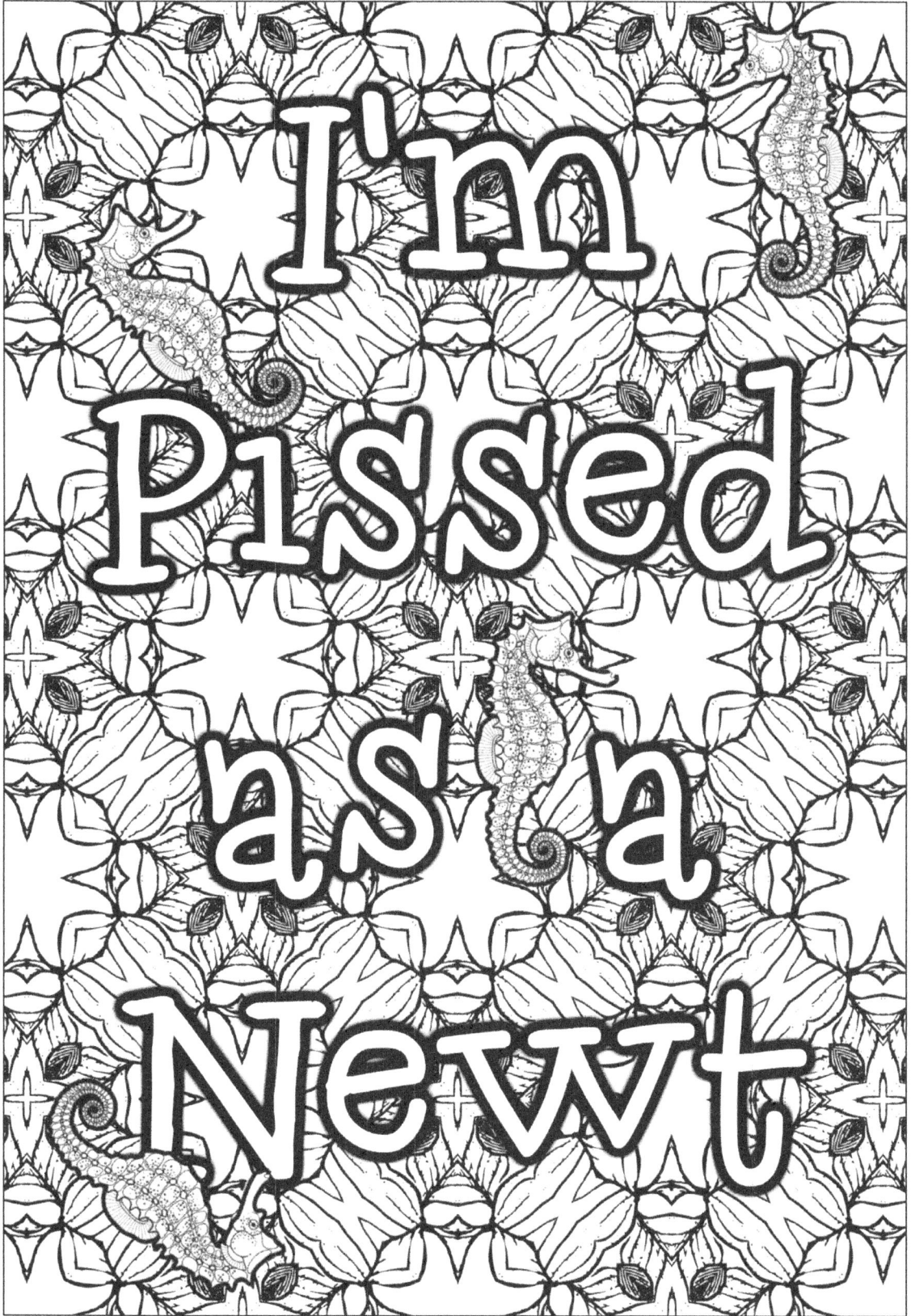

I'm Pissed as a Newt

ill let out your evil soul by incision of steel

You'll go down with the tide

Thou Reeky Fish-Skinned Lout

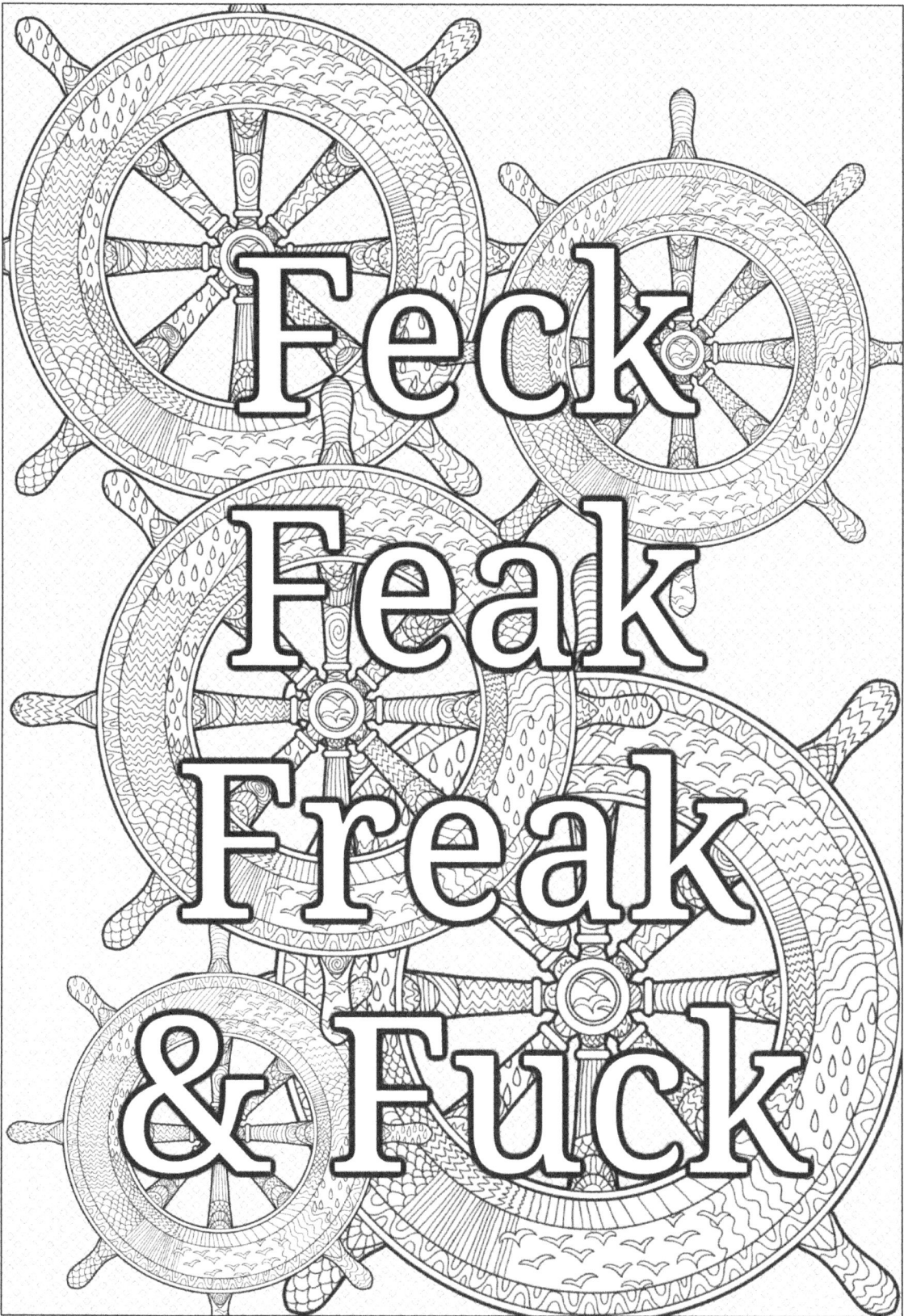

Feck
Feak
Freak
& Fuck

ask my arse

kiss my blind purple cheeks

I'll fly your bloody head as my banner!

You'll rue the day your mother ever spawned you

MAY THE PLAGUE SEIZE YOU

Damn you
to the depths
of the
deepest
darkest
sea

Beezelbub himself

could hardly desire

better company

Here's fine stuff for the gallows

Hold your tongue and your whinin for them thats at your beck and call... because I aint

Yellow
was never
a pirates color

You've got no more brain than a boil on my arse

You should be more a man and less a fish

your minds unhinged

You've neither sense nor memory

Conclusion

I hope you've enjoyed **Pirate Swears**, and if you did, I'd appreciate it if you would leave a review wherever you bought it – this really helps indie authors and artists like me.

Now if you want to REALLY turn the air blue with some more MODERN "colorful" language check out **Southern Swears That'll Get Your Mouth Washed Out with Soap, Mid-Western Swears**, and the **A-Z Book of Inventive Swears**.

Color me impressed!

I ♥ Coloring Books

Made in the USA
Coppell, TX
06 June 2023